BTS

A Little Golden Book® Biography

By Jan Ann • Illustrated by Hyesung Park

A GOLDEN BOOK • NEW YORK

Golden Books
An imprint of Random House Children's Books
A division of Penguin Random House LLC
1745 Broadway, New York, NY 10019
penguinrandomhouse.com
rhcbooks.com
Text copyright © 2025 by Jan Ann
Cover art and interior illustrations copyright © 2025 by Hyesung Park
Golden Books, A Golden Book, A Little Golden Book, the G colophon, and the
distinctive gold spine are registered trademarks of Penguin Random House LLC.
Library of Congress Control Number: 2024949987
ISBN 978-0-593-90442-8 (trade) — ISBN 978-0-593-90443-5 (ebook)
Manufactured in the United States of America
10 9 8 7 6 5 4 3 2 1
EU Contact: Penguin Random House Ireland, 32 Nassau Street, Dublin D02 YH68.
https://eu-contact.penguin.ie

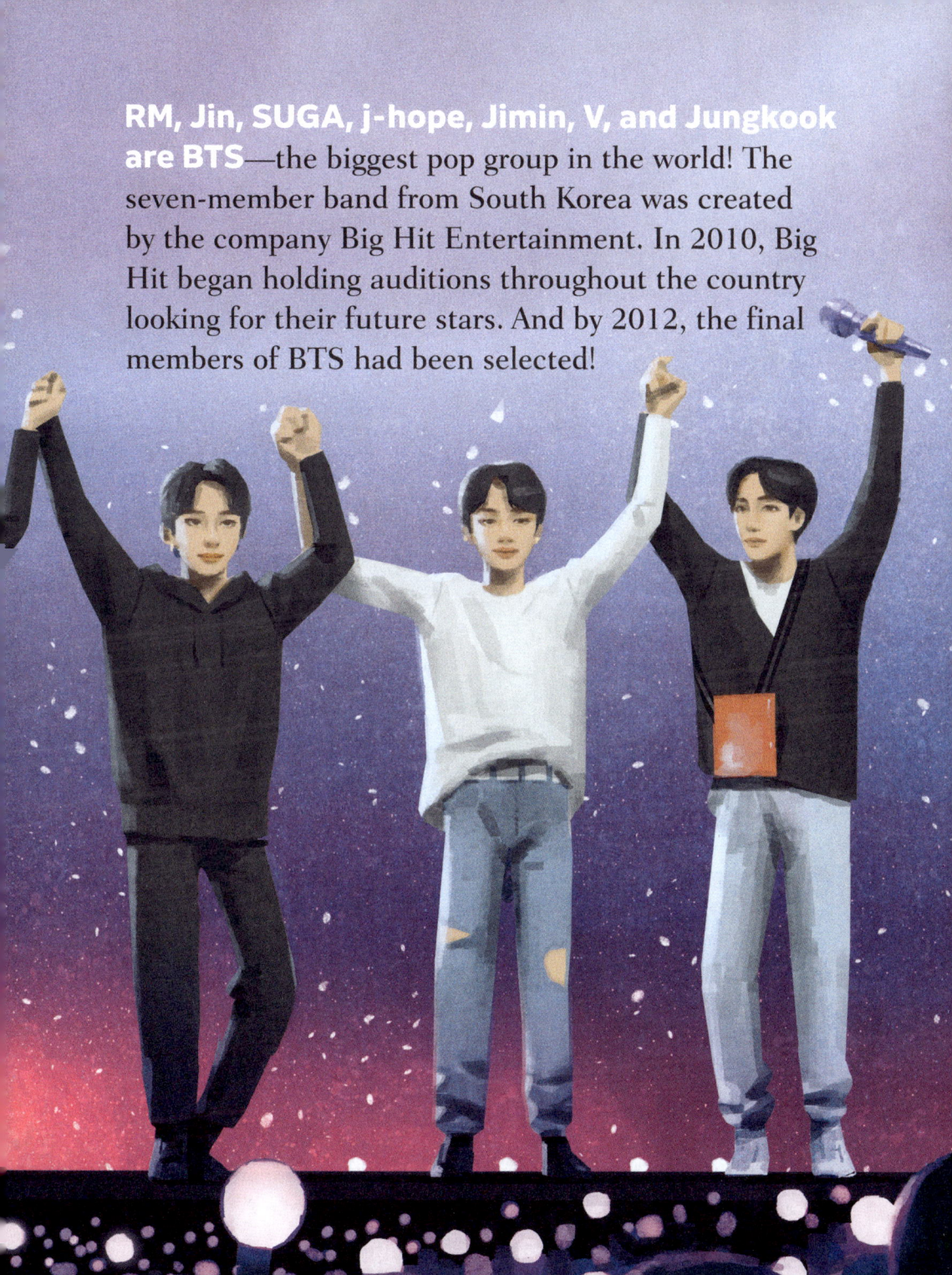

RM, Jin, SUGA, j-hope, Jimin, V, and Jungkook are BTS—the biggest pop group in the world! The seven-member band from South Korea was created by the company Big Hit Entertainment. In 2010, Big Hit began holding auditions throughout the country looking for their future stars. And by 2012, the final members of BTS had been selected!

Kim Nam-joon, now known as RM, was born on September 12, 1994. In the first grade, he started watching documentaries about hip-hop artists and rappers like Nas and Eminem. RM also liked writing poetry. Some of his poems have been turned into songs. He auditioned for Big Hit in 2010 and was the first one picked to join BTS. RM is also the group's leader!

Kim Soek-jin, known as Jin, was born on
December 4, 1992. While in college, Jin studied acting
and developed an interest in music. One day, he was
spotted by a Big Hit talent scout while walking down
the street. The scout noticed his handsome looks and
soon discovered his talent for singing and dancing.

Min Yoon-gi, who would become SUGA, was born on March 9, 1993. He began writing music when he was twelve years old, and by the time he was seventeen, he was earning money as a songwriter. He also began performing as a rapper. He came up with the stage name SUGA by using the first two syllables of the words "shooting guard," the position he played on his high school basketball team.

J-hope was born Jung Ho-seok on February 18, 1994. At the age of ten, he was the youngest student to join the Gwangju Music Academy. As a teenager, he won first place in a national dance competition. After signing with Big Hit, the skilled hip-hop dancer learned how to rap. J-hope chose his stage name to be a source of hope for his fans and bandmates!

Park Ji-min was born on October 13, 1995. Jimin's love for dance started after he joined an after-school break-dancing club. He went on to study contemporary dance in high school, and one of his teachers suggested he audition for an entertainment company. That led Jimin to Big Hit. After joining the company, he also developed his talent for singing!

V was born Kim Tae-hyung on December 30, 1995. While singing in his elementary school talent show, V realized he wanted to be a professional performer. He learned how to play the saxophone and later took dance lessons. When Big Hit held auditions in his city, V went just to support a friend who was trying out. But they asked V to try out, too—and he got picked!

Jeon Jung-kook was born on September 1, 1997. As a child, Jungkook excelled in sports and art but also wanted to be a singer. In 2011, after auditioning for a talent show, Jungkook received offers from seven entertainment companies—including Big Hit! Jungkook chose to sign with Big Hit because he was so impressed with RM's rap skills.

The seven boys lived together in a one-room dormitory while preparing for their debut as a music group. They spent as many as fourteen hours a day practicing rap and hip-hop dancing and writing songs for their album. With a shared goal in mind, they encouraged and supported each other and became good friends as well as a team.

BTS began connecting with their fans online months before their first public appearance as a group. They would talk openly into the camera about what was happening in their lives. Jin posted photos of himself cooking in the dorm, and Jimin shared videos of his dance practices.

V was kept as a secret member to add an extra level of interest to their upcoming debut. He was revealed to the public in a stunning photograph on June 3, 2013.

As they continued to share their lives, they gained more and more fans. BTS's fans would soon become known as ARMY.

On June 13, 2013, the day after the release of
their first album, *2 COOL 4 SKOOL*, BTS debuted
on the South Korean TV show *M Countdown*.

They performed the songs "We Are Bulletproof Pt. 2"
and "No More Dream." The audience loved their amazing
singing, rapping, and spectacular hip-hop dancing.

Some people said the group wouldn't succeed because Big Hit was a small company that didn't have much money to promote them. But that didn't stop BTS. They practiced and wrote music about what was happening in their lives and the struggles facing young people. Their hard work paid off. By early 2014, they had been awarded Best New Artist by three major award shows in South Korea. And that was just the beginning—BTS would go on to win hundreds of awards!

Later that year, they traveled to California to take part in a Korean variety show called *American Hustle Life*. The goal was for BTS to learn about American hip-hop culture from famous hip-hop artists through a series of assignments. One task was to hold a free concert. Jimin, V, and Jungkook handed out flyers, asking people to "please come to our concert." About two hundred people came.

BTS became even more popular with songs such as "Dope," "Run," "Blood Sweat & Tears," and "Spring Day." Their music began to include pop sounds in addition to hip-hop.

In 2017, they were the first Korean artists invited to the American Music Awards. They were greeted by adoring fans and performed their newest song "DNA" to a cheering crowd.

The music video for "DNA" would go on to receive over 1.5 billion views on YouTube, with over six million comments praising BTS and the iconic song!

In 2017, BTS teamed up with UNICEF to launch the Love Myself campaign, inspiring young people to improve their lives by loving themselves. BTS later spoke at the General Assembly of the United Nations. There, RM urged world leaders and fans around the globe to not only love themselves but to speak for themselves. BTS wants everyone to tell their story and be proud of who they are.

BTS continued to release new albums and try new things with their music and performances. They combined Korean instruments with African rhythms and electronic music to create the global sound of their hit song "IDOL."

From small gatherings with dozens of fans in South Korea to a free concert in the United States for a few hundred people to performing at sold-out stadiums around the world, BTS has become more popular than anyone could have imagined.

They hold over twenty-five Guinness World Records, have sold more than forty million physical albums, and are the first group since the Beatles to have three number one albums in less than a year.

As RM, Jin, SUGA, j-hope, Jimin, V, and Jungkook became successful artists, they also became a family. They bonded with each other through their struggles and achievements and shared their lives with their faithful fans, ARMY. BTS's music continues to bring joy to people around the world. What will they do next?

THE BEST IS YET TO COME!